Social Curriculum for TEENS

Job Skills

KRYSTAL GRIFF, MA

Trixie Lulah Publishing

©**Check in with Mrs G LLC**
2020- Present
All Rights Reserved

ISBN: 9798627767826

Vocational Read Aloud:

A Note to Parents & Educators

Dear Parent or Educator,

Thank you for teaching your child to think critically through difficulties they will encounter in the workplace! Social skill are vital to success and happiness both inside and outside of the classroom.

This curriculum helps students prepare for potentially challenging social situations in a safe environment. Model positive problem solving strategies as you discuss how to successfully navigate employment skills.

Enjoy the conversations and connections that will come from these prompts!

Best,

Krystal Griff

checkinwithmrsg.org

Vocational Read Aloud:

Lesson Outline

1. Read the passage aloud

2. Allow student to take notes

3. Use the discussion questions to talk through all sides of the conflict

4. Together, make a decision about how the conflict could be resolved (example solutions are provided for each conflict)

5. Use the "Make a Connection" question to apply the topic to your own life & discuss

Vocational Scenario Topic	Page
Switching Schedules	1-2
Applying for the Same Job	3-4
Boss Blames	5-6
Coworker is Stealing	7-8
Broken Item	9-10
Late for Work	11-12
Paycheck is Too Small	13-14
Unsure	15-16
Boss is in a Meeting	17-18
Rude Customer	19-20
Coworker is Messing Around	21-22
Time is Up	23-24
Boss Asks about Schedule Change	25-26
Friend Applies for a Job	27-28
Not Her Job	29-30
Boss Gives a Compliment	31-32
Coworkers Go to Dinner	33-34
Customer Complains about Change	35-26
Sister is Graduating	37-38
Feeling Sick	39-40

Vocational Read Aloud:
<u>Switching Schedules</u>

Sarah and Janae are friends. They also work together at a grocery store where they are both cashiers. The girls are happiest when they work the same shift. They love to talk to each other between customers.

Their boss posts the new work schedule for the week. Janae is disappointed when she looks at it! Janae's family will be in town on Friday and she wants to go to breakfast with them. But, Janae is scheduled to work on Friday morning.

Janae wants to switch schedules with Sarah so she can have the day off on Friday. Sarah doesn't want to switch schedules because she planned on going to the beach on Friday. Janae thinks that Sarah should go to the beach any other day. Sarah does not feel good about saying no to her friend but, does not want to change her plans.

1

Discussion Questions: Switching Schedules

1. Where do Sarah and Janae work?

2. What is the conflict they are having?

3. Why does Janae want to switch schedules?

4. What does Sarah have planned for Friday?

5. How might Janae be feeling?

6. Who do you think is at fault and why?

7. How do you think they should resolve the conflict?

Suggested Solutions: Switching Schedules

o **Janae should ask her family to meet at a different time so she does not have to switch schedules**

o **Sarah should tell Janae how she feels**

o **Sarah should reschedule her beach trip and help her friend**

o **Janae should apologize for making Sarah uncomfortable and miss seeing her family for breakfast**

Make a Connection: Switching Schedules

What would you do if a friend asked you to switch your day off with theirs and you already had plans?

2

Vocational Read Aloud:
<u>Applying for the Same Job</u>

Brandon and Leo are best friends. They are on summer break from school. Both boys are hoping to get a job for the summer. Brandon sees a posting online for a job at Target. Brandon tells Leo and they both apply for the job. They so excited when they each get an interview!

Leo dresses nicely, practices what he wants to say, and arrives on time for his interview. He answers the questions clearly and shakes the interviewer's hand before he leaves. Brandon is nervous, not prepared, and arrives two minutes late. He stumbles through the interview and does not make a good impression.

Leo gets the job! Brandon feels disappointed that he told Leo about the job posting. Brandon wonders whether or not he would have gotten the job if Leo would not have applied. Leo is wondering why his friend Brandon does not seem to be happy for him.

3

Discussion Questions: Applying for the Same Job

1. How do Brandon and Leo know each other?

2. What is the conflict?

3. Who discovered to job posting?

4. What is one possible reason that Leo may have gotten the job instead of Brandon?

5. Is it reasonable to feel disappointed or jealous when a friend gets something you want?

6. How do you think they should resolve the conflict?

Suggested Solutions: Applying for the Same Job

- ○ **Leo should ask Brandon to be more supportive**

- ○ **Leo should not accept the job since it is making Brandon uncomfortable**

- ○ **Brandon should try to be happy for his friend**

- ○ **Brandon should ask Leo for help with his interviewing skills**

- ○ **Brandon should tell Leo how he is feeling**

Make a Connection: Applying for the Same Job

How would you feel if a friend of yours applied for the job you wanted and got it? What would you say to your friend?

4

Vocational Read Aloud:
Boss Blames

Selena and Travis work at a shoe store that sells athletic shoes. Their job is to stack the shoes neatly in the correct area for each size. Sometimes, boxes are stacked fifteen high!

Today, Travis gets off later than Selena. When Selena leaves, she asks Travis if he can finish stacking the last boxes. Travis says it is no problem. But, when Selena leaves, Travis takes all of the boxes and shoves them messily into one pile. He wants to get home on time. Selena's boss finds the messy stack of shoes.

The next day at work, Selena and Travis are called into a meeting. Their boss tells them that she is disappointed in them and that they will need to fix the shoes as soon as possible. Travis thinks it is no big deal and says that he and Selena will work together to fix the stack. Selena is frustrated because she had nothing to do with the messy stack of shoes. Selena does not want her boss to think that she did not do her job.

Discussion Questions: Boss Blames

1. What is Selena and Travis' job?

2. What is the conflict?

3. Why does Selena feel frustrated?

4. Why do you think Travis tells his boss that he and Selena will work together to fix the shoes?

5. How might Selena's boss be feeling about Selena and Travis?

6. Who do you think is at fault and why?

7. How do you think they should resolve the conflict?

Suggested Solutions: Boss Blames

o **Travis should talk to his boss and tell her that Selena had nothing to do with the messy shoe boxes**

o **Selena should tell her boss that it was Travis' responsibility**

o **Selena should tell Travis that she is frustrated and help him fix the boxes anyway**

o **Travis should apologize to Selena and fix the boxes by himself**

Make a Connection: Boss Blames

How would you feel if your boss blamed you for something you did not do? Would you tell your boss who did it or would you just work to fix it?

6

Vocational Read Aloud:
<u>Coworker is Stealing</u>

Javier and Michael work at a coffee shop. Part of their responsibility is to count the money in the cash register at the end of the day.

The money at the end of every day should be $500. Even though they are supposed to count the money together, Michael always asks Javier to count the money alone. Michael is happy that Javier counts the money alone so that he can clean the floors quickly and they can leave early.

On Sunday night, Javier noticed $20 missing from the register. He documented it for his boss. On Tuesday night, Javier counted the money and found $50 missing. Michael is the only other person with access to the money. Javier wonders if Michael is stealing money from the cash register.

Discussion Questions: Coworker is Stealing

1. Where do Javier and Michael work?

2. What is the conflict?

3. Why is it a good idea for Javier and Michael to count the money together?

4. How much money is missing between Sunday and Tuesday?

5. What could be happening to the money?

6. How do you think they should resolve the conflict?

Suggested Solutions: Coworker is Stealing

o **Javier should confront Michael about the missing money**

o **Javier should call his boss and tell him that he suspects Michael is stealing**

o **Michael and Javier should call their boss together**

o **Michael should count the money instead of Javier**

o **They should each bring money from home to make up the difference from the missing money**

Make a Connection: Coworker is Stealing

What would you do if you found money missing from the cash register at the end of your workday? How would you handle it if you suspected that a coworker maybe stealing the money?

8

Vocational Read Aloud:

<u>Broken Item</u>

Willow works in a little store attached to a gas station. She is stocking the glass drinks in the refrigerated case. Willow notices two ten year old boys running full speed down the aisle.

Willow asks the boy's mother, Mia, to please tell her sons to stop running. Mia is offended and asks Willow to mind her own business.

The two boys swing open the glass door of the refrigerated case and argue over who will take the drink out. The boys slam into each other shouting and grabbing the glass bottles of tea. The boys drop the drink and the glass shatters all over the floor.

Mia feels embarrassed that her sons have broken a bottle and caused a huge mess. Willow feels furious that there is glass all over the store. Willow, Mia, and the two boys stand over the shattered glass.

q

Discussion Questions: Broken Item

1. Where does Willow work?

2. How do Willow and Mia come into contact with each other?

3. What is the conflict?

4. How did the glass get onto the floor?

5. What is one possible reason that Mia was offended by Willow's question?

6. Who do you think is at fault and why?

7. How do you think they should resolve the conflict?

Suggested Solutions: Broken Item

- **Mia should pay for the glass drink**

- **Willow should clean up the mess and not say anything to Mia**

- **Mia should make her boys apologize for the mess**

- **Mia should make her boys help clean up the mess**

- **Willow should scold Mia for not watching her kids in the store**

- **The boys should apologize and take responsibility for their actions**

Make a Connection: Broken Item

What would you do if children were playing rough where you work and created a huge mess? Would you ask them to stop? Would you talk to their parent?

10

Vocational Read Aloud:
Late for Work

Trey works at a bakery downtown. He has to be at work at 5:00am to bake the bread. Trey has trouble waking up in the morning. Trey asks his mom Linda to set her alarm clock and wake him up at 4:30am.

Linda woke up to her alarm ringing at 5:30am. She accidentally set it for the wrong time. She went into Trey's room to find him still asleep. Linda woke Trey up.

Trey was more than an hour late for work and did not get the bread baked on time. Linda feels terrible that Trey was late for work but, she is also wondering why he did not set his own alarm clock. Trey is worried that he will get in trouble with his boss and is angry at his mom for not waking him up on time.

Discussion Questions: Late for Work

1. How do Trey and Linda know each other?

2. Why was Trey late for work?

3. How is Linda feeling?

4. How is Trey feeling?

5. What do you think Trey should say when his boss asks him why he is late for work?

6. Who do you think is at fault and why?

7. How do you think they should resolve the conflict?

Suggested Solutions: Late for Work

- **Trey should be responsible for getting himself to work on time**

- **Trey should apologize to his boss and to Linda**

- **Linda should apologize to Trey for setting her alarm clock incorrectly**

- **Linda should call Trey's boss and explain that it was her fault**

Make a Connection: Late for Work

What would you woke up late and knew that you would not make it to work on time?

12

Paycheck is Too Small

Sam works as a dog groomer. She gets paid every $200 every week. Today, Sam's boss Tom asked her to stay all day to help him with five extra dog washing appointments. Sam's boss is always helpful, so Sam agreed to stay. She worked four more hours than usual. Sam was excited for the extra money should would get on her paycheck.

When she picks up her paycheck on Friday, Sam is surprised to see that it is only her usual $200. Sam feels unsure of whether or not she should ask Tom to pay her for the extra hours she worked on Tuesday.

She hopes that it was a mistake and that Tom will notice it on his own. Tom forgot that he asked Sam to stay and does not realize that there is a problem with her paycheck. Sam feels resentful that she did not get paid for the extra hours she worked.

13

Discussion Questions: Paycheck is Too Small

1. Where does Sam work?

2. What is the conflict?

3. Why did Sam work extra hours on Tuesday?

4. Why didn't Tom pay her for her extra time?

5. How might Tom be feeling?

6. How do you think they should resolve the conflict?

Suggested Solutions: Paycheck is Too Small

- Sam should ask Tom to pay her for the extra hours

- Tom should review his paychecks to make sure all of his employees are paid the right amount

- Sam should not say anything and never work extra hours again

Make a Connection: Paycheck is Too Small

What would you do if your paycheck was smaller than expected?

14

Vocational Read Aloud:
Unsure

Joe works at a clothing store. He is busy folding shirts on the sales floor. Joe's boss Kora walks up to him quickly. She is talking loud and fast. She tells Joe that he needs to go into the backroom and steam all of the blue jackets right away. Joe can tell that Kora is stressed out. Joe wants to help and be a good employee so he says, "Ok! No problem!".

Once Kora walks away, Joe realizes that he is unsure of how to operate the steamer. Joe goes into the back room and spends 15 minutes trying to figure out how to use it with no luck. He did not want to ask Kora to help him because she was already so busy.

Kora comes into the backroom expecting the blue jackets to be steamed. Joe is embarrassed that he was not able to operate the steamer. Kora is frustrated with Joe.

15

Discussion Questions: Unsure

1. Where does Joe work?

2. How do Kora and Joe know each other?

3. How does Joe know that Kora is stressed out?

4. Why do you think Joe did not want to ask Kora for help when he was unsure of how to use the steamer?

5. Why do you think Kora was frustrated with Joe?

6. How do you think they should resolve the conflict?

Suggested Solutions: Unsure

- Joe should apologize to Kora and ask her to show him how to use the steamer

- Kora should apologize to Joe for being too stressed out to help

- Joe should tell Kora that steaming things is not his job

- Kora should train all of her employees on how to use the steamer

- Next time Joe should ask for help right away

- Next time Kora should slow down and make sure Joe knows what she is asking him to do

Make a Connection: Unsure

What would you do if your boss asked you to quickly do a task that you were unsure of how to complete?

16

Vocational Read Aloud:
<u>Boss is in a Meeting</u>

Josh works at the customer service desk at a computer store. One of his coworkers is sick, so he is working alone.

There is a line of nine customers waiting for his help. Josh is working with each customer as fast as he can. A customer named Nicole walks up to the service desk and yells, "This is ridiculous! I just need one thing. You need to help me now. I am not waiting!" Josh says politely, "Please wait in line I will help you as soon as I can." Nicole snapped, "I want to talk to your boss NOW!".

Josh looked at the schedule and knew that his boss was in a meeting. Josh was unsure of whether or not he should interrupt his bosses meeting and of what he should say to the customer.

Discussion Questions: Boss is in a Meeting

1. What kind of work does Josh do at the computer store?

2. What is the conflict?

3. Why is there such a long line at the customer service desk?

4. Do you think Josh's boss would want to be interrupted to talk to this customer?

5. Is it reasonable to demand to talk to someone's boss?

6. How do you think they should resolve the conflict?

Suggested Solutions: Boss is in a Meeting

○ **Josh should stop helping customers and get his boss**

○ **Nicole should apologize and get back in line**

○ **Josh should give out his bosses phone number and ask Nicole to call him later**

○ **Nicole should write her complaint and leave it for Josh's boss**

○ **Josh should ask one of his coworkers to talk to Nicole**

Make a Connection: Boss is in a Meeting

What would you do if a customer demanded to talk to your boss while your boss was in a meeting?

18

Vocational Read Aloud:
<u>Rude Customer</u>

Khloe works at a sandwich shop. Khloe greets the next customer, Leah, with her friendly smile. Leah works at a phone store across the street and eats lunch at the sandwich shop almost everyday.

Today Leah looks unfriendly and does not smile at Khloe. Leah orders her sandwich and taps her foot while she waits to receive it. Khloe makes the sandwich and hands it to Leah. Leah takes her sandwich and sits down quickly. After one bite, she walks up to the counter and shouts, "This sandwich is a mess! It is sloppy and I want a new one now!".

Khloe feels upset that Leah is yelling at her. Khloe thought that they were becoming friends. Leah is upset too but Khloe is unsure of why.

Discussion Questions: Rude Customer

1. How do Leah and Khloe know each other?

2. What is the conflict?

3. How do you think Leah's day was before she walked into the sandwich shop?

4. What is Leah's complaint about the sandwich?

5. Is there anything that Khloe could have done differently?

6. Who do you think is at fault and why?

7. How do you think they should resolve the conflict?

Suggested Solutions: Rude Customer

o **Leah should apologize to Khloe**

o **Khloe should smile and make Leah a new sandwich**

o **Leah should tell Khloe why she was frustrated in a nice way**

o **Khloe should tell Leah how she is feeling after being yelled at**

Make a Connection: Rude Customer

How would you feel if a customer you knew came into your work and yelled at you for no reason? What would you say to the customer?

20

Coworker is Messing Around

Jared and Megan work at a hardware store. They both love their jobs and try to make working as enjoyable as possible for each other.

Jared is asked to restock the wood. He walked to the wood pile and began to stack it with wood from the backroom. Megan saw Jared and said she would help.

But, when Megan got to the wood pile she picked up one of the long sticks and started to play baseball with the wood. She tried to make Jared join in on her game. Jared was nervous because he wanted to get his job done. Megan told Jared that he is boring and that working with him was not fun.

Discussion Questions: Coworker is Messing Around

1. Where do Megan and Jared work?

2. How do Megan and Jared feel about their jobs?

3. What is the conflict?

4. Is there a difference between making your job enjoyable and messing around too much?

5. How do you think Megan might be feeling when she decides to play baseball with the wood?

6. How do you think they should resolve the conflict?

Suggested Solutions: Coworker is Messing Around

- **Megan should apologize to Jared and help him stack the wood**

- **Jared should tell his boss and stack the wood alone**

- **Jared should apologize to Megan for being uptight**

Make a Connection: Coworker is Messing Around

How would you react if a coworker was pressuring you to mess around at work instead of getting your job done?

22

Vocational Read Aloud:
<u>Time is Up</u>

Jake is the manager at pizza restaurant. He is very organized and likes things to be clean and put away. Jake makes a list of things for each of his employees to complete everyday.

Francisco works for Jake and always does his best while he is at work. Today, Francisco gets a list with three things on it from Jake. Jake wants Francisco to clean the sink, mop the floors and dust the plants.

Francisco starts on his list when he notices that the floors are extra dirty. Francisco spends two hours cleaning the floors. When he is done he realizes it is already time for him to go home. Francisco is wondering if he should stay longer to finish the list Jake gave him. Jake is wondering why the sink is still dirty and the plants have not been dusted.

Discussion Questions: Time is Up

1. How do Jake and Francisco know each other?

2. What is the conflict?

3. How do you think Francisco is feeling at the end of his shift?

4. If Francisco stays to finish his list, Jake will have to pay him for working the extra hours. How do you think Jake is feeling?

5. Who do you think is at fault and why?

6. How do you think they should resolve the conflict?

Suggested Solutions: Time is Up

o **Jake should ask Francisco to stay and agree to pay him for the extra hours**

o **Francisco should apologize for not completing the list and ask a coworker to finish the tasks for him**

o **Francisco should thank Jake for doing such a thorough job on the floors. Francisco should agree to manage his time better in the future.**

Make a Connection: Time is Up

What would you do if your boss gave you a list to complete and you were unable to finish it before your shift was over?

24

Vocational Read Aloud:
<u>Boss Asks for a Schedule Change</u>

Amelia works at a fast food restaurant. Her boss Eva always schedules Amelia from 10:00am-2:00pm on Thursdays because Amelia has a college math class at 2:30pm on Thursdays.

Today is Thursday, Amelia has a ton of math homework to turn in. She is looking forward to getting off of work. It is 1:45pm Eva notices that there are 26 customers coming into the restaurant and even more in the drive thru. Eva asks Amelia to stay for an extra hour and help.

Amelia does not want to be late for her math class. Eva is not sure how she will help all of the customers if Amelia leaves on time.

Discussion Questions: Boss Asks for a Schedule Change

1. Where do Eva and Amelia work?

2. How do Eva and Amelia know each other?

3. What is the conflict?

4. Why did Eva ask Amelia to stay?

5. Why is it a tough decision for Amelia?

6. How do you think Amelia felt when Eva asked her to stay?

7. Who do you think is at fault and why?

8. How do you think they should resolve the conflict?

Suggested Solutions: Boss Asks for a Schedule Change

○ **Amelia should apologize to Eva and go to her math class on time.**

○ **Eva should not have asked Amelia to stay. So, Eva should apologize to Amelia and make the customers wait.**

○ **Amelia should compromise and stay for a few minutes longer than her shift.**

○ **Eva should tell Amelia to go home now before it gets too busy.**

Make a Connection: Boss Asks for a Schedule Change

What would you do if your boss asked you to stay longer than your scheduled shift? Would it make a difference whether or not you had something important to do after work?

26

Friend Applies for a Job

Lincoln's parents own a car dealership. They want him to work there for the summer. Lincoln is playing high school football and thinks that he is too busy to work.

Lincoln tells his best friend Tyler about the job at his parent's company. Tyler applies for the job even though he also plays football. Tyler is hired by Lincoln's parents right away. Lincoln's parents are so proud of Tyler and the work Tyler is doing with their company.

Lincoln is a little jealous of the way his parents are talking about Tyler. Tyler is excited to have a good summer job and is saving all of the money he makes. Lincoln and Tyler feel a little uncomfortable around each other at football practice.

Discussion Questions: Friend Applies for a Job

1. How do Tyler and Lincoln know each other?

2. How did Tyler find out about the job at the car dealership?

3. What is the conflict?

4. Why do you think Lincoln's parents are proud of Tyler?

5. Why do you think Tyler and Lincoln are feeling a little uncomfortable around each other?

6. How do you think they should resolve the conflict?

Suggested Solutions: Friend Applies for a Job

○ **Lincoln should talk to his parents and see if there is a way he can work at their company with Tyler.**

○ **Tyler should ask Lincoln why he is feeling jealous since he passed on the job.**

○ **Tyler and Lincoln should agree to keep their friendship and football practice separate from Tyler's job.**

Make a Connection: Friend Applies for a Job

How would you feel if a friend of yours took a job that you passed on? Would it be difficult to see them being successful in that position?

28

Vocational Read Aloud:
<u>Not Her Job</u>

Ellie and Brianna are coworkers at a library downtown. Ellie is in charge of putting all of the returned books back onto the shelves in the correct places. Brianna is in charge of reading books to kids during the library's Story Time Events.

Ellie is doing her job, she has four more shelves of books to organize before she leaves. Brianna walks quickly around the corner and says to Ellie, "You need to do Story Time for me. I have so much going on and there are kids waiting." Brianna does not wait for Ellie to respond.

Ellie has never done Story Time and is not interested in learning to do it. Brianna feels that she is too busy to take the time to read to kids. There are three kids waiting at the carpet for Story Time to start. Ellie is unsure of where Brianna went when she walked away.

29

Discussion Questions: Not Her Job

1. How do Brianna and Ellie know each other?

2. Who is in charge of the Story Time Events?

3. What is the conflict?

4. Why does Brianna think Ellie should do Story Time?

5. How might Ellie be feeling about the way Brianna talked to her?

6. How do you think they should resolve the conflict?

Suggested Solutions: Not Her Job

- **Brianna should apologize for being rude to Ellie and do her own job**

- **Brianna should ask for help instead of demanding it**

- **Ellie should stop what she is doing and help Brianna**

- **Ellie should talk to Brianna about how she is feeling**

- **Ellie should talk to her manager**

Make a Connection: Not Her Job

How would you respond to a coworker who asked you to complete a task that was not your job?

30

Vocational Read Aloud:
<u>Boss gives a Compliment</u>

David works at an ambulance company. Each day he is in charge of washing all of the ambulances inside and out. He restocks all of the medical supplies inside and is sure to check the tires.

Wednesday, when David arrived at work he found that Michelle, who does his job on his days off, had already completed all of the tasks. Every single ambulance was ready to go!

When David's boss Hector arrived, he noticed the good work. Hector thanked David for doing such a wonderful job of cleaning the ambulances. Hector told David that he should teach Michelle how to be as efficient as he was.

David felt uncomfortable taking credit for Michelle's work but, David did not tell Hector that Michelle is the one who completed everything. When Michelle arrived at work, Hector told her how much he appreciated all of the work David had done.

31

Discussion Questions: Boss gives a Compliment

1. What is the conflict?

2. Why do you think David took credit for Michelle's work?

3. How do you think Michelle felt when Hector told her about all the work "David" had done?

4. What should David have said to Hector?

5. What might happen if David is asked to train Michelle?

6. How do you think they should resolve the conflict?

Suggested Solutions: Boss gives a Compliment

- David should tell Hector that Michelle is the one who completed the work

- Michelle should tell Hector that she is the one who completed the work

- Hector should ask Michelle and David how they feel about their work before asking David to train Michelle

- David and Michelle should move on without talking about it

Make a Connection: Boss gives a Compliment

How would you feel if your boss complimented you for something you did not do? Would you tell your boss that you did not do it?

32

Vocational Read Aloud:
<u>Coworkers go to Dinner</u>

Jennifer is a receptionist at a doctors office. She works with seven other busy receptionists. Jennifer feels that her coworkers are her friends.

During her break Jennifer walks into the lunch room and finds her coworker Ben showing pictures on his phone from a dinner at his house the night before. Jennifer notices that all of her coworkers are in the photos except for her.

Ben tells Jennifer that he had a small dinner party and did not invite her because he thought she would be too busy to attend. Jennifer's feelings are hurt. She would have loved to spend time with her coworkers outside of work. She wonders whether or not they enjoy working with her. Ben feels awkward.

Discussion Questions: Coworkers go to Dinner

1. How do Jennifer and Ben know each other?

2. What is the conflict?

3. How might this affect Jennifer and Ben's relationship at work?

4. How do you think Jennifer and Ben's coworkers who are in the lunchroom are feeling?

5. Who is at fault?

6. How should they resolve the conflict?

Suggested Solutions: Coworkers go to Dinner

- Ben should apologize to Jennifer

- Ben should ask Jennifer whether or not she would like to come to the next party he has

- Jennifer should tell Ben that next time she would like to come to his party

- Jennifer should talk to her coworkers about Ben and his party

- Jennifer should act like she did not want to attend the party

Make a Connection: Coworkers go to Dinner

How would you feel if found out that all of your coworkers went to dinner without you? Would your feelings affect your ability to work with your coworkers?

34

Customer Complains about Change

Monique works as a cashier. She likes her job because she gets to talk with lots of people. One of her favorite customers is an old man named Gary. Gary comes in each morning to buy chocolate milk.

Today, Gary paid for his chocolate milk with a five dollar bill. Monique counted out his change as she does everyday. She tried to hand him the $3.50 she owed him. But, Gary insisted that he paid with a ten dollar bill and that he should get five more dollars back as change.

Monique is 100% sure that Gary paid with a five dollar bill and that she has given him the correct change. Gary is 100% sure that he has given Monique a ten dollar bill. Monique and Gary are unsure of what to do.

Discussion Questions: Customer Complains

1. What is the conflict between Monique and Gary?

2. Where are Monique and Gary?

3. What is the relationship between Monique and Gary?

4. How do you think Monique is feeling about Gary?

5. How might Gary be feeling about Monique?

6. How do you think they should resolve the conflict?

Suggested Solutions: Customer Complains

○ Monique should count the register at the end of the night and if there is an extra $5 she should call Gary and apologize

○ Gary should apologize to Monique and assume that he gave her $5

○ Monique should ask her manger to take a look at the register

○ Gary should double check his wallet to see which of this bills he used

Make a Connection: Customer Complains

What would you do if a customer insisted that you gave them the wrong amount of change? How would you resolve the conflict?

36

Vocational Read Aloud:
Sister is Graduating

Isaiah works as a personal trainer at a gym. He has many clients that only want to meet with him. Isaiah does his best to give exceptional customer service by working around his clients' schedules.

One of his best clients, Abby, wants to schedule time with Isaiah on Sunday morning. Isaiah never works on Sundays, but without looking at his schedule, Isaiah says yes. On Saturday night, Isaiah remembers that his little sister is graduating from high school on Sunday morning.

He is unsure of what to do. Isaiah does not want to miss the graduation but, he also does not want to disappoint Abby by cancelling her appointment the night before.

Discussion Questions: Sister is Graduating

1. Where does Isaiah work?

2. What conflict is Isaiah having?

3. How might Abby react if Isaiah cancels her appointment the night before?

4. How might Isaiah's little sister feel if Isaiah misses her high school graduation?

5. How do you think he should resolve the conflict?

Suggested Solutions: Sister is Graduating

- Isaiah should cancel on Abby

- Isaiah should skip his sister's graduation

- Isaiah should ask Abby if there is another time that would work for her

Make a Connection: Sister is Graduating

What would you do if you accidentally double booked yourself with work and a personal event? How would you decide which to cancel?

Vocational Read Aloud:
Feeling Sick

Liam and Kayden work as tellers at the bank. They take turns going into work early in the morning to open the bank.

It is Kayden's turn to open the bank. He wakes up and is not feeling well. Kayden is unsure of whether or not he will be able to work today. Kayden calls Liam and asks if he can open the bank, this is the fifth time Kayden has asked Liam to open the bank for him.

Liam does not want to go to work early. He had a late night and was looking forward to sleeping in. Liam tells Kayden that he is tired and does not want to go. Kayden feels nauseous and thinks Liam should help him out. Liam feels that Kayden maybe faking a sickness and is not feeling sympathetic towards him. The bank needs to be opened in the next thirty minutes. Liam and Kaden are both feeling frustrated.

39

Discussion Questions: Explain Yourself

1. How do Liam and Kayden know each other?

2. Whose responsibility is it to open the bank today?

3. Why does Kayden call Liam?

4. How might Liam's reaction have been different if this was the first time Kayden had asked him to open the bank?

5. How do you think they should resolve the conflict?

Suggested Solutions: Explain Yourself

○ **Kayden should open the bank and if he is still not feeling well he should go back home**

○ **Liam should help Kayden by opening the bank for him**

○ **Kayden should call his manager and have his manager ask Liam to open the bank**

○ **Liam and Kayden should talk to each other about trust so they can develop a better working relationship**

Make a Connection: Explain Yourself

What would you do if a coworker repeatedly called in sick leaving you to fill in for them? How would it make you feel? How would you feel if you were too sick to work and no one was available to work for you?

40

About the Author:

Krystal Griff, MA is the founder of Check in with Mrs G LLC. She is a Special Education Teacher & Mom who has been teaching social skills for over 10 years. She creates curriculum to empower students in the classroom and at home.

Read More:

- o checkinwithmrsg.org

Connect:

- o Email: checkinwithmrsgontpt@gmail.com
- o Instagram: @checkinwithmrs_g
- o Facebook: @checkinwithmrsgontpt

Made in the USA
Coppell, TX
28 October 2023